Air Traffic Control

Contents

By Carol Krueger

Air Traffic Control

PREDICT What information do you think you will find out about?

Every day, worldwide, thousands of aircraft fly from airport to airport, carrying millions of passengers. With the help of air traffic controllers, these planes are able to fly at the same time without crashing into each other, reaching their destinations safely.

Air traffic controllers act as the eyes and ears of the pilots, making sure that planes keep a safe distance from each other. They talk to the pilots over the radio, telling them what speed and height to fly at in order to travel safely over long distances, even in cloud or at night.

Air traffic controllers work with computers and radar to co-ordinate and control the movements of all of the planes in their area and keep them separated. They tell them when they can take off, keep them safe in the air and guide them in to land on the runway. They are able to help pilots avoid bad weather or bumpy turbulence, and keep the aircraft traffic flowing smoothly.

Los Angeles International Airport

CLARIFY

co-ordinate

turbulence

air traffic control tower at Reagan National Airport, Virginia, USA

thousands of aircraft . . .
. . . millions of passengers

WORD ORIGIN

radar

Where's it from?

Air traffic controllers use radar to help them track the planes.

QUESTION

Why do you think the sky would need to be divided into airspaces?

Air traffic controllers work together as a team.

Controlling the Airspace

The sky is divided into invisible sections called airspaces. The air traffic controllers work together like a basketball team, with each member of the team looking after the planes in their airspace. Once a plane has flown through a controller's airspace and is about to leave it, the controller passes the plane on to another controller on the team.

Air traffic controllers have to be able to think in three dimensions — up and down, sideways and up close and far away. They also have to make decisions quickly because planes fly very fast and, unlike cars, they can't just stop and wait while a controller decides where they should fly next. This means that controllers have to have an excellent knowledge of their section of airspace and the flying characteristics of all the planes flying within it.

INFERENCE

What can you infer about the type of person an air traffic controller might need to be?

As they work, the air traffic controllers gather information from what they hear over the radio and what they can see on the radar screen. They need to know how to read and interpret symbols and predict where an aircraft will be at any time from the plane's current course and speed. Their computers help them detect if planes are flying too close together, or if a plane is descending too low for safety. The computers send out an alert telling them to direct the plane elsewhere.

By using these skills and computer systems, air traffic controllers can track planes in the sky, pinpointing exactly the position of all the planes that are flying, at any time, all of the time. Air traffic controllers have to be able to concentrate and focus on what they're doing and not be distracted by anything. The safety of all the people flying in the planes inside their section of airspace depends on them.

QUESTION

What types of symbols do you think air traffic controllers would need to interpret?

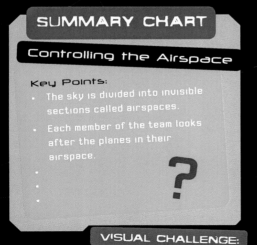

SUMMARY CHART

Controlling the Airspace

Key Points:
- The sky is divided into invisible sections called airspaces.
- Each member of the team looks after the planes in their airspace.
-
-

?

VISUAL CHALLENGE:

In what other ways could you show this information?

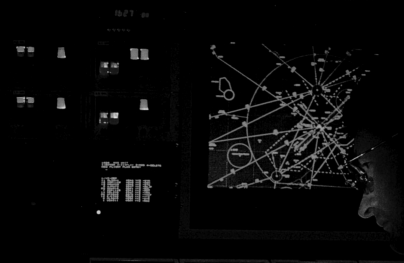

an air traffic controller handling flight data at
Pearson International Airport, Ontario, Canada

pinpointing exactly the position
of all the planes

INFERENCE

**What can you infer
about the importance of
computers and radar when
tracking planes?**

needed to reach an alternative airport in an emergency.

Flights monitored by air traffic control follow particular routes, called airways, which are also noted in the flight plan. Within these airways, pilots also have to maintain the correct altitude, or "flight level". This helps ensure there is no risk of a mid-air collision.

The flight plan also includes the estimated duration of the flight, what type of flight it is and the number of passengers on board.

The flight plans are filed by pilots with the local Aviation Authority and are entered into the air traffic control computer system. The computer then sends the flight plan information to all the controllers monitoring the airspace between the airport where the plane is due to take off and its destination.

When making a flight plan, there are many checkpoints to be made.

INFERENCE

What can you infer about the importance of a flight plan?

Before a plane can take off, pilots need to file a flight plan that is entered into the air traffic control computer system.

CLARIFY

flight plan
monitored
duration

a copy of a pilot's flight plan log

370 486   124   037   005
020 476   124   0874 0172

VGFR   ACTUAL G/S....
370 482   124   000   000
020 476   124   0874 0172

370 482   124   103   012
020 476   124   0771 01

UAL G/S.

jet fuel being pumped into a plane

Summary Chart

Before the Flight

?

Key Points

?

The pilot calls the airport's control tower for route clearance.

The pilot files a flight plan showing the intended route.

Visual Challenge: In what other ways could you show this information?

Once the passengers and crew are on board and all flight checks are completed, the passenger airbridge can be removed, and the doors closed.

cargo being loaded onto a plane

With the flight plan filed and pre-flight checks underway, the pilot calls the airport's control tower for route clearance. The control tower confirms the cruise altitude for the flight and the "squawk" code, which is entered into the plane's transponder system. The squawk code is the flight's unique identifier. The plane's transponder constantly transmits the code and it is picked up on radar by the controllers monitoring the flight.

Deciding on a specific cruise altitude depends on the type of aircraft and weather information. Both the pilot and first officer on the plane will have calculated the fastest and most fuel-efficient cruise altitude for the trip, and the likely flight time. They also take into account the comfort of the passengers and use weather information they receive to stay away from any turbulence in the sky.

Once route clearance has been received, the plane has been loaded with baggage and freight and all the passengers and crew are on board, the plane doors are closed and the aircraft is ready to go. The pilot calls the control tower to confirm the number of passengers and crew on the flight, and request clearance to start the engines.

QUESTION

Why do you think the number of passengers and crew on the flight needs to be confirmed with the control tower?

Leaving the Airport

The Tower Controller either gives clearance for the plane to start its engines or tells the pilot to wait. They tell the pilot to wait if there is already a line of aircraft on the taxiway waiting for take-off clearance and several aircraft on their final approach for landing. The controller will then advise an engine start clearance time. If they know there will be a delay, the flight crew can save fuel by not starting the engines until they know they're about to depart.

Other factors can also delay take-off. Turbulence and bad weather can cause slippery runways and poor visibility, and planes have to taxi and land more slowly.

Once the control tower gives engine start clearance, the ground tug pushes the aircraft away from the bridge and the engines are started. When the ground tug disengages from the plane and the pilot has completed the flight deck checks, they call the tower for taxi clearance.

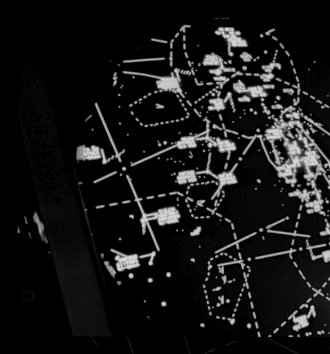

WORD ORIGIN

engine

Where's it from?

Ground tugs are used to push and tow aircraft when needed.

The pilot completes the flight deck check and calls the tower for taxi clearance.

CLARIFY

taxiway
tug
disengages

13

INFERENCE

What can you infer about the importance of the "holding point" on a runway?

the air tower clears
the l...ke...ff...

QUESTION GENERATE

What questions could you ask?

Air traffic controllers handle incoming and departing planes at Auckland Airport, New Zealand.

a holding point on a runway

The Tower Controller clears the aircraft and confirms which runway to use, depending on the wind direction. The controller also assigns the plane a "holding point". This is a marked section on the taxiway at the ent to the runway, where the plane will wait to take off. The controller also advises the pilot of any other aircraft or vehicle ground movements that may affect the plane's tax to the runway.

The plane then taxies away from the termi along the taxiway. While this is happening there may be aircraft ahead getting ready to take off and other aircraft coming in to land. Over the cabin's loudspeakers, the pi welcomes passengers on board, and gives details of the flight time and cruise height, and tells them where the plane is in the queue for departure.

The air tower clears the flight for take-off and outlines which direction to fly and at what altitude, taking into account any oth air traffic in the area.

Summary Chart

Leaving the Airport

Key Points:

- The Tower Controller either gives clearance for the plane to start its engines or tells the pilot to wait.
-
-
-

?

Visual Challenge:

In what other ways could you show this information?

High in the sky ∎⁻⌐

When the plane has taken off and the landing gear has been raised, the first officer radios an Approach Radar Controller. These controllers manage an airspace around the airport called the Terminal Control Area, which is used by aircraft approaching or leaving the airport. It normally covers a circle of about 40 nautical miles out, reaching up between 6500 and 9500 feet.

The first officer confirms the plane is airborne and gives the flight number and the altitude the aircraft is passing as it climbs to its cruise altitude. The Approach Radar Controller identifies the aircraft on the radar screen and confirms this with the flight deck. The controller then clears the aircraft, passing on any altitude restrictions. Altitude restrictions are holding points at certain heights that the plane cannot go above until cleared by the controller. This helps ensure that the plane does not climb to its cruise altitude before the airspace above it is clear of other aircraft.

CLARIFY

**nautical miles
restrictions**

confirms the plane is airborne

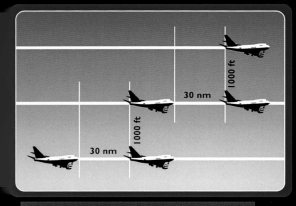

FERENCE

...an you infer from ...
...e must be a safe
...e between them...?

...there is bad weather

Separation between planes needs to be 1000 feet
vertically and 30 nautical miles horizontally.

1000 ft

30 nm

1000 ft

30 nm

CLARIFY

extent
congestion

As the flight progresses, the pilot is instructed to change their radio frequency to that of the Area Radar Controllers. When it has reached its cruise altitude, the plane enters a new airspace, which is split into sectors. Each sector is handled by a different area controller. The size of each sector is determined by the expected amount of air traffic within it and factors such as the extent of radar coverage.

As planes fly to their different destinations, there must be a safe distance between them. This is called safe separation and the controllers are responsible for this. Sometimes, when there is heavy traffic or bad weather, the pilot may have to change the original flight plan. The controllers are able to guide the plane around bad weather and away from traffic congestion. If there is a lot of wind turbulence, the pilot may ask the controllers for a change in altitude. This will either reduce or avoid the turbulence and make travel more comfortable for the passengers.

While the aircraft flies to its destination, watched by the controllers, the cabin crew make sure the passengers are comfortable. Usually the passengers give little thought to the work going on behind the scenes and the procedures required to keep them travelling at high speeds far above the Earth.

QUESTION GENERATE

What questions could you ask about this information?

Coming Down

As the plane nears the airport, the first officer stays in contact with the Area Radar Controller. If there is another in-bound flight, the plane may be given a new course for its approach to the runway. This will maintain the required separation "buffer" between the two planes.

As aircraft approach their destinations, the separation buffers that keep them from colliding get smaller. The plane is now back in the hands of an Approach Radar Controller, who will work with the various flight crews to keep safe distances between all the planes as they near the airport and help them line up for the runway.

With only a few kilometres to go to the airport, the flight is passed on from the airport's Approach Radar Controller to the control tower for its final descent and landing clearance. A smooth and gradual descent shoud be all the passengers notice as the plane lines up for landing.

. . . line up
for the runway . . .

QUESTION

What do you think could happen if communication between the plane and the air traffic controllers was lost?

WORD ORIGIN

colliding

Where's it from?

A plane that is about to land descends over city buildings.

Arriving
at the Airport

If there are too many planes arriving at the airport at the same time, the plane may have to wait its turn to land. This is very different from a traffic jam on a road. Planes can't stop and wait as cars can, so the air traffic controllers direct incoming planes to fly in a tall, circular pattern in a holding area away from the runway.

This patterned approach is called "stacking" and each aircraft flies as part of this pattern, following another plane as it circles. The planes peel off from the bottom of the stack, one by one, as they are given clearance by the controller to begin their final approach to land. As each plane leaves the stack, the others spiral down a level, until it is the next plane's turn to land.

The pilot then illuminates the seatbelt light and the cabin crew check the passengers to make sure everyone is belted in safely for landing.

QUESTION GENERATE

What questions could you ask?

22

CLARIFY

peel off

5000 feet

4000 feet

3000 feet

2000 feet

Stacking pattern – planes need to stay 1000 feet
above one another as they wait to land

... scans the sky for each plane

A plane parked at a terminal gate is being
cleared of luggage, refuelled and cleaned.

ground staff directing a plane

The Tower Controller scans the sky for planes using binoculars. As each little black dot is spotted in the sky beyond the far end of the runway, the controller quickly and expertly checks the sky around it and the runway to ensure the route ahead is clear. The pilot is then given clearance to land. The controller also monitors the spaces between the aircraft and any other landing planes ahead or behind it to make sure it has plenty of time to exit the runway before the next plane lands.

When the plane touches down and the pilot applies the airbrakes to slow the plane, it is passed on to the Ground Controller, who monitors the runways, taxiways and terminal apron, guiding the plane to the correct terminal gate. The airport's ground staff help the pilot to park the aircraft at its gate, using hand signals. The cleaning, fuel and baggage tenders arrive ready to prepare the plane for its next flight.

CLARIFY

terminal apron

tenders

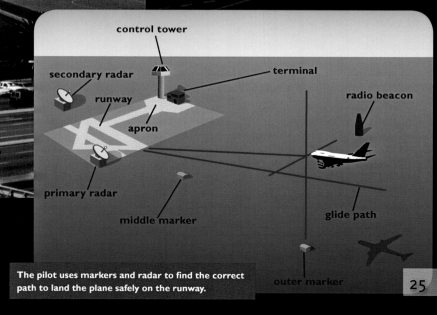

The pilot uses markers and radar to find the correct path to land the plane safely on the runway.

As they prepare to leave the plane, most passengers give little thought to the many air traffic controllers who have worked to ensure that they arrive safely. But the controllers have no time to congratulate themselves on a job well done – they are busy with the planes that have just arrived in their airspace, making sure they arrive safely, too. Whenever people fly, whatever the weather, day or night, air traffic controllers are working to keep them safe.

OPINION

Has your opinion of flying and the importance of air traffic control changed? Why/why not?

SUMMARY CHART

Air Traffic Control

Key Points:
*
*
*
*
*
*
*

?

VISUAL CHALLENGE:

In what other ways could you show this information?

Check In
Departures
Lost property
← North terminal
Trains

← Coach station
Courtesy coaches
Taxis
Car parks
Car rental

P & O Airport Assistance
Hotel Inn →

INDEX

Think
about the
Text

Making connections — what connections can you make to the information presented in Air Traffic Control?

making difficult decisions

interpreting information

solving problems

Text
to
Self

being able to work under pressure

working as a team

protecting something

to
ext

er informational texts
read that have similar
pare the texts.

Text to
World

Talk about situations in the world
that might connect to elements in
the text.

Planning an Informational Report

1 ORGANISE THE INFORMATION

SELECT A TOPIC:

Air Traffic Control

WHAT I KNOW:

- Air traffic controllers work at airports.
- They help pilots take off, fly and land safely.
- There are different types of air traffic controllers, who do different jobs.

WHAT I WILL RESEARCH:

- What are the roles of the different air traffic controllers?
- How do they work with the flight crew?
- What equipment do they use?

2 LOCATE THE INFORMATION YOU WILL NEED

→ library

→ Internet

→ experts

3 PROCESS THE INFORMATION

Skim-read.
Sort your ideas into groups.
Make some headings.

4 PLAN THE REPORT

Write a general introduction.

5 DECIDE ON A LOGICAL ORDER FOR YOUR INFORMATION

What will come first, next ... last?

6 WRITE UP YOUR INFORMATION

7 DESIGN SOME VISUALS TO INCLUDE IN YOUR REPORT

You can use graphs, diagrams, labels, charts, tables, cross-sections ...

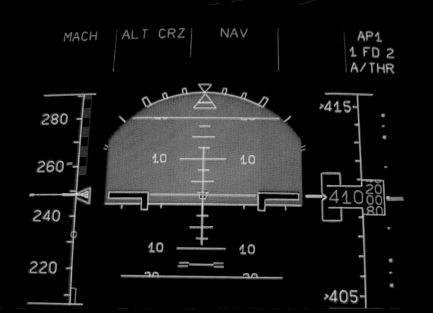

Writing an Informational Report

Have you . . .

- recorded important information?

- written in a formal style that is concise and accurate?

- avoided unnecessary descriptive details, metaphors or similes?

- used scientific or technical terms?

- written a logical sequence of facts?

- avoided author bias or opinion?

DON'T FORGET to revisit your writing. Do you need to change, add or delete anything to improve your report?